This journal belongs to:

_____

ONE Question A DAY for Moms

A FIVE-YEAR JOURNAL

Daily Reflections on Motherhood

Castle Point Books
New York

ONE QUESTION A DAY FOR MOMS.
Copyright © 2019 by St. Martin's Press.

All rights reserved. Printed in Turkey.

For information, address St. Martin's Press,
175 Fifth Avenue, New York, N.Y. 10010.

www.castlepointbooks.com
www.stmartins.com

The Castle Point Books trademark is owned by Castle Point Publishing, LLC.
Castle Point books are published and distributed by St. Martin's Press, LLC.

Flower illustrations on cover and interior © Shutterstock.com
Additional cover illustrations by Young Jin Lim

ISBN 978-1-250-20231-4 (trade paperback)

Our books may be purchased in bulk for promotional, educational, or business use.
Please contact your local bookseller or the Macmillan Corporate and Premium Sales Department
at 1-800-221-7945, extension 5442, or by email at MacmillanSpecialMarkets@macmillan.com.

First Edition: March 2019

10 9 8 7 6 5 4 3

PARENTING IS AN ADVENTURE

like no other, but it goes by much too fast.

One Question a Day for Moms allows you to create

a time capsule of your experience as a mother and

preserve memories that are too precious to leave behind.

Enter the current year on the line provided and jot down

the first answer that comes to mind. As the years go by,

you'll have created a story that spans five years and a

family keepsake that's yours to treasure forever.

January 1

What is one parenting goal you have?

Year: _____ _____

_____

_____

_____

Year: _____ _____

_____

_____

_____

Year: _____ _____

_____

_____

_____

Year: _____ _____

_____

_____

_____

Year: _____ _____

_____

_____

_____

January 2

What is the best part about being a mom?

Year: _____ _____
_____
_____
_____

Year: _____ _____
_____
_____
_____

Year: _____ _____
_____
_____
_____

Year: _____ _____
_____
_____
_____

Year: _____ _____
_____
_____
_____

January 3

What is one goal you have for your family?

Year: _____ _____

_____

_____

_____

Year: _____ _____

_____

_____

_____

Year: _____ _____

_____

_____

_____

Year: _____ _____

_____

_____

_____

Year: _____ _____

_____

_____

_____

January 4

What should every mom carry in her purse?

Year: _____ _____

_____

_____

Year: _____ _____

_____

_____

Year: _____ _____

_____

_____

Year: _____ _____

_____

_____

Year: _____ _____

_____

_____

January 5

What mom inspires you, and why?

Year: _____ _____

_____

_____

_____

Year: _____ _____

_____

_____

_____

Year: _____ _____

_____

_____

_____

Year: _____ _____

_____

_____

_____

Year: _____ _____

_____

_____

_____

January 6

What do you love about your life?

Year: _____ _____

_____

_____

_____

Year: _____ _____

_____

_____

_____

Year: _____ _____

_____

_____

_____

Year: _____ _____

_____

_____

_____

Year: _____ _____

_____

_____

_____

January 7

What makes you most proud of your children?

Year: _____ _____

_____

_____

_____

Year: _____ _____

_____

_____

_____

Year: _____ _____

_____

_____

_____

Year: _____ _____

_____

_____

_____

Year: _____ _____

_____

_____

_____

January 8

What parenting tricks have you picked up?

Year: _____ _____

_____

_____

_____

Year: _____ _____

_____

_____

_____

Year: _____ _____

_____

_____

_____

Year: _____ _____

_____

_____

_____

Year: _____ _____

_____

_____

_____

January 9

What is a common phrase your kids hear from you?

Year: _____ _____

_____

_____

_____

Year: _____ _____

_____

_____

_____

Year: _____ _____

_____

_____

_____

Year: _____ _____

_____

_____

_____

Year: _____ _____

_____

_____

_____

January 10

What was the last thing your child did/said
that made you laugh?

Year: _____ _____

_____

_____

_____

Year: _____ _____

_____

_____

_____

Year: _____ _____

_____

_____

_____

Year: _____ _____

_____

_____

_____

Year: _____ _____

_____

_____

_____

January 11

What is your ideal vacation?

Year: _____ _____
_____
_____
_____

Year: _____ _____
_____
_____
_____

Year: _____ _____
_____
_____
_____

Year: _____ _____
_____
_____
_____

Year: _____ _____
_____
_____
_____

January 12

If you could get a few hours to yourself
today, what would you do?

Year: _____ _____

_____

_____

_____

Year: _____ _____

_____

_____

_____

Year: _____ _____

_____

_____

_____

Year: _____ _____

_____

_____

_____

Year: _____ _____

_____

_____

_____

January 13

What is the most important lesson your
kids have learned?

Year: _____ _____

_____

_____

_____

Year: _____ _____

_____

_____

_____

Year: _____ _____

_____

_____

_____

Year: _____ _____

_____

_____

_____

Year: _____ _____

_____

_____

_____

January 14

What is the most important lesson your
kids are still learning?

Year: _____ _____

_____

_____

_____

Year: _____ _____

_____

_____

_____

Year: _____ _____

_____

_____

_____

Year: _____ _____

_____

_____

_____

Year: _____ _____

_____

_____

_____

January 15

How have you changed as a mom this year?

Year: _____   _____

_____

_____

_____

Year: _____   _____

_____

_____

_____

Year: _____   _____

_____

_____

_____

Year: _____   _____

_____

_____

_____

Year: _____   _____

_____

_____

_____

January 16

The hardest thing about being a mom is _____.

Year: _____ _____
_____
_____
_____

Year: _____ _____
_____
_____
_____

Year: _____ _____
_____
_____
_____

Year: _____ _____
_____
_____
_____

Year: _____ _____
_____
_____
_____

January 17

If your child were a color, what color would he/she be?

Year: _____ _____

_____

_____

Year: _____ _____

_____

_____

Year: _____ _____

_____

_____

Year: _____ _____

_____

_____

Year: _____ _____

_____

_____

January 18

What have you recently learned about yourself?

Year: _____   _____

_____

_____

_____

Year: _____   _____

_____

_____

_____

Year: _____   _____

_____

_____

_____

Year: _____   _____

_____

_____

_____

Year: _____   _____

_____

_____

_____

January 19

I love it when my kids _____.

Year: _____   _____

_____

_____

_____

Year: _____   _____

_____

_____

_____

Year: _____   _____

_____

_____

_____

Year: _____   _____

_____

_____

_____

Year: _____   _____

_____

_____

_____

January 20

Whose parenting style differs most from yours?

Year: _____ _____
_____
_____
_____

Year: _____ _____
_____
_____
_____

Year: _____ _____
_____
_____
_____

Year: _____ _____
_____
_____
_____

Year: _____ _____
_____
_____
_____

January 21

What memories have you made this year?

Year: _____ _____

_____

_____

_____

Year: _____ _____

_____

_____

_____

Year: _____ _____

_____

_____

_____

Year: _____ _____

_____

_____

_____

Year: _____ _____

_____

_____

_____

January 22

When was the last time you were embarrassed?

Year: _____ _____

_____

_____

Year: _____ _____

_____

_____

Year: _____ _____

_____

_____

Year: _____ _____

_____

_____

Year: _____ _____

_____

_____

January 23

What have you said that sounded a lot
like your own mom?

Year: _____ _____

_____

_____

_____

Year: _____ _____

_____

_____

_____

Year: _____ _____

_____

_____

_____

Year: _____ _____

_____

_____

_____

Year: _____ _____

_____

_____

_____

January 24

When was the last time you slept in past 9 a.m.?

Year: _____ _____
_____
_____
_____

Year: _____ _____
_____
_____
_____

Year: _____ _____
_____
_____
_____

Year: _____ _____
_____
_____
_____

Year: _____ _____
_____
_____
_____

January 25

What is your child's spirit animal?

Year: _____ _____
_____
_____
_____

Year: _____ _____
_____
_____
_____

Year: _____ _____
_____
_____
_____

Year: _____ _____
_____
_____
_____

Year: _____ _____
_____
_____
_____

January 26

When was the last time you stayed up past midnight?

Year: _____ _____

_____

_____

_____

Year: _____ _____

_____

_____

_____

Year: _____ _____

_____

_____

_____

Year: _____ _____

_____

_____

_____

Year: _____ _____

_____

_____

_____

January 27

What is your greatest accomplishment?

Year: _____ _____
_____
_____
_____

Year: _____ _____
_____
_____
_____

Year: _____ _____
_____
_____
_____

Year: _____ _____
_____
_____
_____

Year: _____ _____
_____
_____
_____

January 28

I have come to realize I need _____.

Year: _____ _____

_____

_____

_____

Year: _____ _____

_____

_____

_____

Year: _____ _____

_____

_____

_____

Year: _____ _____

_____

_____

_____

Year: _____ _____

_____

_____

_____

January 29

Name one way in which you've changed
since becoming a mom.

Year: _____ _____

_____

_____

_____

Year: _____ _____

_____

_____

_____

Year: _____ _____

_____

_____

_____

Year: _____ _____

_____

_____

_____

Year: _____ _____

_____

_____

_____

January 30

What keeps you sane on the craziest of days?

Year: _____ _____

_____

_____

Year: _____ _____

_____

_____

Year: _____ _____

_____

_____

Year: _____ _____

_____

_____

Year: _____ _____

_____

_____

January 31

Describe a heartwarming moment you
recently enjoyed with your kids.

Year: _____ _____

_____

_____

_____

Year: _____ _____

_____

_____

_____

Year: _____ _____

_____

_____

_____

Year: _____ _____

_____

_____

_____

Year: _____ _____

_____

_____

_____

February 1

What is your new favorite song?

Year: _____ _____

_____

_____

_____

Year: _____ _____

_____

_____

_____

Year: _____ _____

_____

_____

_____

Year: _____ _____

_____

_____

_____

Year: _____ _____

_____

_____

_____

February 2

What is the best movie you've seen in a long time?

Year: _____ _____

_____

_____

Year: _____ _____

_____

_____

Year: _____ _____

_____

_____

Year: _____ _____

_____

_____

Year: _____ _____

_____

_____

February 3

Which sitcom most resembles your life?

Year: _____ _____

_____

_____

_____

Year: _____ _____

_____

_____

_____

Year: _____ _____

_____

_____

_____

Year: _____ _____

_____

_____

_____

Year: _____ _____

_____

_____

_____

February 4

How long would you last trying to survive in the wild?

Year: _____ _____
_____
_____

Year: _____ _____
_____
_____
_____

Year: _____ _____
_____
_____

Year: _____ _____
_____
_____

Year: _____ _____
_____
_____

February 5

What compliment do you frequently get from people?

Year: _____ _____

_____

_____

_____

Year: _____ _____

_____

_____

_____

Year: _____ _____

_____

_____

_____

Year: _____ _____

_____

_____

_____

Year: _____ _____

_____

_____

_____

February 6

What is something unique about you?

Year: _____ _____

_____

_____

Year: _____ _____

_____

_____

Year: _____ _____

_____

_____

Year: _____ _____

_____

_____

Year: _____ _____

_____

_____

February 7

What is something unique about your family?

Year: _____ _____

_____

_____

_____

Year: _____ _____

_____

_____

_____

Year: _____ _____

_____

_____

_____

Year: _____ _____

_____

_____

_____

Year: _____ _____

_____

_____

_____

February 8

What fictional character does your child most remind you of?

Year: _____   _____

_____

_____

_____

Year: _____   _____

_____

_____

_____

Year: _____   _____

_____

_____

_____

Year: _____   _____

_____

_____

_____

Year: _____   _____

_____

_____

_____

February 9

What do you do better than any mom you know?

Year: _____ _____

_____

_____

_____

Year: _____ _____

_____

_____

_____

Year: _____ _____

_____

_____

_____

Year: _____ _____

_____

_____

_____

Year: _____ _____

_____

_____

_____

February 10

What was the last event you were happy to skip?

Year: _____ _____

_____

_____

_____

Year: _____ _____

_____

_____

_____

Year: _____ _____

_____

_____

_____

Year: _____ _____

_____

_____

_____

Year: _____ _____

_____

_____

_____

February 11

What do you most enjoy doing with friends?

Year: _____ _____

_____

_____

_____

Year: _____ _____

_____

_____

_____

Year: _____ _____

_____

_____

_____

Year: _____ _____

_____

_____

_____

Year: _____ _____

_____

_____

_____

February 12

Where does your family most often gather in your home?

Year: _____ _____

_____

_____

_____

Year: _____ _____

_____

_____

_____

Year: _____ _____

_____

_____

_____

Year: _____ _____

_____

_____

_____

Year: _____ _____

_____

_____

_____

February 13

What have your kids taught you recently?

Year: _____ _____

_____

_____

_____

Year: _____ _____

_____

_____

_____

Year: _____ _____

_____

_____

_____

Year: _____ _____

_____

_____

_____

Year: _____ _____

_____

_____

_____

February 14

What makes you feel loved?

Year: _____   _____

_____

_____

_____

Year: _____   _____

_____

_____

_____

Year: _____   _____

_____

_____

_____

Year: _____   _____

_____

_____

_____

Year: _____   _____

_____

_____

_____

February 15

What brings you back to your own childhood?

Year: _____ _____

_____

_____

Year: _____ _____

_____

_____

Year: _____ _____

_____

_____

Year: _____ _____

_____

_____

Year: _____ _____

_____

_____

February 16

Describe your best friend.

Year: _____ _____

_____

_____

_____

Year: _____ _____

_____

_____

_____

Year: _____ _____

_____

_____

_____

Year: _____ _____

_____

_____

_____

Year: _____ _____

_____

_____

_____

February 17

What is the best thing about the town or city where you live?

Year: _____ _____
_____
_____
_____

Year: _____ _____
_____
_____
_____

Year: _____ _____
_____
_____
_____

Year: _____ _____
_____
_____
_____

Year: _____ _____
_____
_____
_____

February 18

Describe your relationship with your child/children.

Year: _____ _____

_____

_____

_____

Year: _____ _____

_____

_____

_____

Year: _____ _____

_____

_____

_____

Year: _____ _____

_____

_____

_____

Year: _____ _____

_____

_____

_____

February 19

If you could be any age, what age would you be?

Year: _____ _____
_____
_____
_____

Year: _____ _____
_____
_____
_____

Year: _____ _____
_____
_____
_____

Year: _____ _____
_____
_____
_____

Year: _____ _____
_____
_____
_____

February 20

How do you envision your future relationship
with your child/children?

Year: _____ _____

_____

_____

_____

Year: _____ _____

_____

_____

_____

Year: _____ _____

_____

_____

_____

Year: _____ _____

_____

_____

_____

Year: _____ _____

_____

_____

_____

February 21

What is your family's favorite meal?

Year: _____ _____

_____

_____

_____

Year: _____ _____

_____

_____

_____

Year: _____ _____

_____

_____

_____

Year: _____ _____

_____

_____

_____

Year: _____ _____

_____

_____

_____

February 22

What is your favorite meal?

Year: _____ _____

_____

_____

_____

Year: _____ _____

_____

_____

_____

Year: _____ _____

_____

_____

_____

Year: _____ _____

_____

_____

_____

Year: _____ _____

_____

_____

_____

February 23

What would be the cherry on top of this day?

Year: _____ _____
_____
_____
_____

Year: _____ _____
_____
_____
_____

Year: _____ _____
_____
_____
_____

Year: _____ _____
_____
_____
_____

Year: _____ _____
_____
_____
_____

February 24

What activity do you most enjoy doing with your child?

Year: _____ _____

_____

_____

_____

Year: _____ _____

_____

_____

_____

Year: _____ _____

_____

_____

_____

Year: _____ _____

_____

_____

_____

Year: _____ _____

_____

_____

_____

February 25

Being a mom has made me a better _____.

Year:_____   _____

_____

_____

_____

Year:_____   _____

_____

_____

_____

Year:_____   _____

_____

_____

_____

Year:_____   _____

_____

_____

_____

Year:_____   _____

_____

_____

_____

February 26

What transition have your kids experienced
this year? How did they handle it?

Year: _____ _____

_____

_____

_____

Year: _____ _____

_____

_____

_____

Year: _____ _____

_____

_____

_____

Year: _____ _____

_____

_____

_____

Year: _____ _____

_____

_____

_____

February 27

What is the best book (or article) you've read recently?

Year: _____ _____

_____

_____

_____

Year: _____ _____

_____

_____

_____

Year: _____ _____

_____

_____

_____

Year: _____ _____

_____

_____

_____

Year: _____ _____

_____

_____

_____

February 28

What personal struggles have you faced in your life?

Year: _____ _____

_____

_____

_____

Year: _____ _____

_____

_____

_____

Year: _____ _____

_____

_____

_____

Year: _____ _____

_____

_____

_____

Year: _____ _____

_____

_____

_____

March 1

How does your partner support you?

Year: _____   _____

_____

_____

_____

Year: _____   _____

_____

_____

_____

Year: _____   _____

_____

_____

_____

Year: _____   _____

_____

_____

_____

Year: _____   _____

_____

_____

_____

March 2

Where would you take your family if
money weren't an obstacle?

Year: _____ _____

_____

_____

_____

Year: _____ _____

_____

_____

_____

Year: _____ _____

_____

_____

_____

Year: _____ _____

_____

_____

_____

Year: _____ _____

_____

_____

_____

march 3

What have you said or done lately
that you wish you hadn't?

Year: _____ _____

_____

_____

_____

Year: _____ _____

_____

_____

_____

Year: _____ _____

_____

_____

_____

Year: _____ _____

_____

_____

_____

Year: _____ _____

_____

_____

_____

March 4

When were you proud of your parenting skills?

Year: _____ _____

_____

_____

_____

Year: _____ _____

_____

_____

_____

Year: _____ _____

_____

_____

_____

Year: _____ _____

_____

_____

_____

Year: _____ _____

_____

_____

_____

March 5

What is the best advice you've received lately?

Year: _____ _____

_____

_____

Year: _____ _____

_____

_____

Year: _____ _____

_____

_____

Year: _____ _____

_____

_____

Year: _____ _____

_____

_____

march 6

What is the best advice you've given lately?

Year: _____ _____

_____

_____

_____

Year: _____ _____

_____

_____

_____

Year: _____ _____

_____

_____

_____

Year: _____ _____

_____

_____

_____

Year: _____ _____

_____

_____

_____

What unwanted or unhelpful advice have you received
from friends, family, or perfect strangers?

Year: _____ _____

_____

_____

_____

Year: _____ _____

_____

_____

_____

Year: _____ _____

_____

_____

_____

Year: _____ _____

_____

_____

_____

Year: _____ _____

_____

_____

_____

March 8

What do you wish you could go back in time to tell yourself?

Year: _____ _____

_____

_____

_____

Year: _____ _____

_____

_____

_____

Year: _____ _____

_____

_____

_____

Year: _____ _____

_____

_____

_____

Year: _____ _____

_____

_____

_____

March 9

Who or what defines your support system?

Year: _____ _____
_____
_____
_____

Year: _____ _____
_____
_____
_____

Year: _____ _____
_____
_____
_____

Year: _____ _____
_____
_____
_____

Year: _____ _____
_____
_____
_____

march 10

What are your wishes for your child/children?

Year: 2022   It's my first day back at work after mat leave. I wish for Kaia to know herself & discover her passions → dharma + a full-filling career + life.

Year: _____ _____

Year: _____ _____

Year: _____ _____

Year: _____ _____

March 11

If you could start your own business, what would it be?

Year: _____ _____
_____
_____
_____

Year: _____ _____
_____
_____
_____

Year: _____ _____
_____
_____
_____

Year: _____ _____
_____
_____
_____

Year: _____ _____
_____
_____
_____

march 12

Being a mom requires _____.

Year: _____ _____
_____
_____
_____

Year: _____ _____
_____
_____
_____

Year: _____ _____
_____
_____
_____

Year: _____ _____
_____
_____
_____

Year: _____ _____
_____
_____
_____

March 13

What is the best part of your day with your children?

Year: _____ _____

_____

_____

_____

Year: _____ _____

_____

_____

_____

Year: _____ _____

_____

_____

_____

Year: _____ _____

_____

_____

_____

Year: _____ _____

_____

_____

_____

March 14

What tough decision have you made lately?
How did it turn out?

Year: _____ _____

_____

_____

_____

Year: _____ _____

_____

_____

_____

Year: _____ _____

_____

_____

_____

Year: _____ _____

_____

_____

_____

Year: _____ _____

_____

_____

_____

March 15

What other roles do you enjoy in addition
to your role as parent?

Year: _____   _____

_____

_____

_____

Year: _____   _____

_____

_____

_____

Year: _____   _____

_____

_____

_____

Year: _____   _____

_____

_____

_____

Year: _____   _____

_____

_____

_____

March 16

What is your idea of success?

Year: _____ _____

_____

_____

_____

Year: _____ _____

_____

_____

_____

Year: _____ _____

_____

_____

_____

Year: _____ _____

_____

_____

_____

Year: _____ _____

_____

_____

_____

march 17

What is your dream job?

Year: _____ _____

_____

_____

_____

Year: _____ _____

_____

_____

_____

Year: _____ _____

_____

_____

_____

Year: _____ _____

_____

_____

_____

Year: _____ _____

_____

_____

_____

march 18

What surprises has life handed you?

Year: _____ _____

_____

_____

_____

Year: _____ _____

_____

_____

_____

Year: _____ _____

_____

_____

_____

Year: _____ _____

_____

_____

_____

Year: _____ _____

_____

_____

_____

march 19

What have you done for yourself lately?

Year: _____ _____

_____

_____

Year: _____ _____

_____

_____

Year: _____ _____

_____

_____

Year: _____ _____

_____

_____

Year: _____ _____

_____

_____

march 20

What three words would you use
to describe your partner?

Year: _____ _____

_____

_____

_____

Year: _____ _____

_____

_____

_____

Year: _____ _____

_____

_____

_____

Year: _____ _____

_____

_____

_____

Year: _____ _____

_____

_____

_____

March 21

What makes you and your partner a good team?

Year: _____   _____

_____

_____

Year: _____   _____

_____

_____

Year: _____   _____

_____

_____

Year: _____   _____

_____

_____

Year: _____   _____

_____

_____

March 22

How do you resolve problems in your family?

Year: _____ _____

_____

_____

_____

Year: _____ _____

_____

_____

_____

Year: _____ _____

_____

_____

_____

Year: _____ _____

_____

_____

_____

Year: _____ _____

_____

_____

_____

march 23

How appreciated do you feel today?

Year: _____ _____

_____

_____

_____

Year: _____ _____

_____

_____

_____

Year: _____ _____

_____

_____

_____

Year: _____ _____

_____

_____

_____

Year: _____ _____

_____

_____

_____

march 24

How do you picture your life changing
over the next ten years?

Year: _____ _____

_____

_____

_____

Year: _____ _____

_____

_____

_____

Year: _____ _____

_____

_____

_____

Year: _____ _____

_____

_____

_____

Year: _____ _____

_____

_____

_____

March 25

What qualities have your kids inherited from you?

Year: _____   _____

_____

_____

_____

Year: _____   _____

_____

_____

_____

Year: _____   _____

_____

_____

_____

Year: _____   _____

_____

_____

_____

Year: _____   _____

_____

_____

_____

march 26

What qualities have your kids inherited
from your partner?

Year: _____ _____

_____

_____

_____

Year: _____ _____

_____

_____

_____

Year: _____ _____

_____

_____

_____

Year: _____ _____

_____

_____

_____

Year: _____ _____

_____

_____

_____

March 27

How would you feel if you found out
you were pregnant today?

Year: _____ _____

_____

_____

_____

Year: _____ _____

_____

_____

_____

Year: _____ _____

_____

_____

_____

Year: _____ _____

_____

_____

_____

Year: _____ _____

_____

_____

_____

march 28

When I look back on the birth of my child . . .

Year: _____ _____

_____

_____

Year: _____ _____

_____

_____

Year: _____ _____

_____

_____

Year: _____ _____

_____

_____

Year: _____ _____

_____

_____

March 29

What do you wish someone had told you about
pregnancy or new parenthood?

Year: _____ _____

_____

_____

_____

Year: _____ _____

_____

_____

_____

Year: _____ _____

_____

_____

_____

Year: _____ _____

_____

_____

_____

Year: _____ _____

_____

_____

_____

March 30

What are you still learning about motherhood?

Year: _____ _____

_____

_____

_____

Year: _____ _____

_____

_____

_____

Year: _____ _____

_____

_____

_____

Year: _____ _____

_____

_____

_____

Year: _____ _____

_____

_____

_____

March 31

What was the last thing you won?

Year: _____ _____

_____

_____

_____

Year: _____ _____

_____

_____

_____

Year: _____ _____

_____

_____

_____

Year: _____ _____

_____

_____

_____

Year: _____ _____

_____

_____

_____

April 1

One misconception I had about this stage
of parenting was _____.

Year: _____   _____

_____

_____

_____

Year: _____   _____

_____

_____

_____

Year: _____   _____

_____

_____

_____

Year: _____   _____

_____

_____

_____

Year: _____   _____

_____

_____

_____

April 2

What age do you like most (for each of your kids)?

Year: _____ _____

_____

_____

_____

Year: _____ _____

_____

_____

_____

Year: _____ _____

_____

_____

_____

Year: _____ _____

_____

_____

_____

Year: _____ _____

_____

_____

_____

April 3

Describe your last moms' night out.

Year: _____ _____

_____

_____

_____

Year: _____ _____

_____

_____

_____

Year: _____ _____

_____

_____

_____

Year: _____ _____

_____

_____

_____

Year: _____ _____

_____

_____

_____

April 4

What is something you have done as a parent that
you never thought you would do?

Year: _____ _____

_____

_____

_____

Year: _____ _____

_____

_____

_____

Year: _____ _____

_____

_____

_____

Year: _____ _____

_____

_____

_____

Year: _____ _____

_____

_____

_____

April 5

My child gets excited when . . .

Year:_____   _____

_____

_____

_____

Year:_____   _____

_____

_____

_____

Year:_____   _____

_____

_____

_____

Year:_____   _____

_____

_____

_____

Year:_____   _____

_____

_____

_____

April 6

This is one of my pet peeves:

Year: _____ _____

_____

_____

_____

Year: _____ _____

_____

_____

_____

Year: _____ _____

_____

_____

_____

Year: _____ _____

_____

_____

_____

Year: _____ _____

_____

_____

_____

April 7

What do you want to remember about today?

Year: _____ _____

_____

_____

_____

Year: _____ _____

_____

_____

_____

Year: _____ _____

_____

_____

_____

Year: _____ _____

_____

_____

_____

Year: _____ _____

_____

_____

_____

April 8

What are you saving for?

Year: _____ _____

_____

_____

_____

Year: _____ _____

_____

_____

_____

Year: _____ _____

_____

_____

_____

Year: _____ _____

_____

_____

_____

Year: _____ _____

_____

_____

_____

April 9

How well do you express your feelings?

Year: _____ _____

_____

_____

_____

Year: _____ _____

_____

_____

_____

Year: _____ _____

_____

_____

_____

Year: _____ _____

_____

_____

_____

Year: _____ _____

_____

_____

_____

April 10

How well do your kids express their feelings?

Year: _____ _____
_____
_____
_____

Year: _____ _____
_____
_____
_____

Year: _____ _____
_____
_____
_____

Year: _____ _____
_____
_____
_____

Year: _____ _____
_____
_____
_____

April 11

What worries you?

Year: _____ _____

_____

_____

_____

Year: _____ _____

_____

_____

_____

Year: _____ _____

_____

_____

_____

Year: _____ _____

_____

_____

_____

Year: _____ _____

_____

_____

_____

April 12

What fear have you conquered?

Year: _____ _____
_____
_____
_____

Year: _____ _____
_____
_____
_____

Year: _____ _____
_____
_____
_____

Year: _____ _____
_____
_____
_____

Year: _____ _____
_____
_____
_____

April 13

My partner and I see eye-to-eye on this issue:

Year: _____ _____

_____

_____

_____

Year: _____ _____

_____

_____

_____

Year: _____ _____

_____

_____

_____

Year: _____ _____

_____

_____

_____

Year: _____ _____

_____

_____

_____

April 14

My partner and I disagree about this a lot:

Year: _____ _____

_____

_____

Year: _____ _____

_____

_____

Year: _____ _____

_____

_____

Year: _____ _____

_____

_____

Year: _____ _____

_____

_____

April 15

What bores you to tears?

Year: _____ _____

_____

_____

_____

Year: _____ _____

_____

_____

_____

Year: _____ _____

_____

_____

_____

Year: _____ _____

_____

_____

_____

Year: _____ _____

_____

_____

_____

April 16

I am so glad _____ is in my kids' lives.

Year: _____   _____
_____
_____
_____

Year: _____   _____
_____
_____
_____

Year: _____   _____
_____
_____
_____

Year: _____   _____
_____
_____
_____

Year: _____   _____
_____
_____
_____

April 17

Who do you miss, and why?

Year: _____   _____

_____

_____

_____

Year: _____   _____

_____

_____

_____

Year: _____   _____

_____

_____

_____

Year: _____   _____

_____

_____

_____

Year: _____   _____

_____

_____

_____

April 18

For what modern invention are you most grateful?

Year: _____ _____

_____

_____

Year: _____ _____

_____

_____

Year: _____ _____

_____

_____

Year: _____ _____

_____

_____

Year: _____ _____

_____

_____

April 19

How do you comfort your kids?

Year: _____ _____

_____

_____

_____

Year: _____ _____

_____

_____

_____

Year: _____ _____

_____

_____

_____

Year: _____ _____

_____

_____

_____

Year: _____ _____

_____

_____

_____

April 20

Don't mess with me when I'm _____.

Year: _____ _____
_____
_____
_____

Year: _____ _____
_____
_____
_____

Year: _____ _____
_____
_____

Year: _____ _____
_____
_____
_____

Year: _____ _____
_____
_____
_____

April 21

When was the last time you dressed up?

Year: _____   _____

_____

_____

_____

Year: _____   _____

_____

_____

_____

Year: _____   _____

_____

_____

_____

Year: _____   _____

_____

_____

_____

Year: _____   _____

_____

_____

_____

April 22

What is your favorite family ritual?

Year: _____ _____

_____

_____

_____

Year: _____ _____

_____

_____

_____

Year: _____ _____

_____

_____

_____

Year: _____ _____

_____

_____

_____

Year: _____ _____

_____

_____

_____

April 23

Who is your kindred spirit?

Year: _____ _____
_____
_____
_____

Year: _____ _____
_____
_____
_____

Year: _____ _____
_____
_____
_____

Year: _____ _____
_____
_____
_____

Year: _____ _____
_____
_____
_____

April 24

What is difficult to admit to yourself or others?

Year: _____ _____

_____

_____

_____

Year: _____ _____

_____

_____

_____

Year: _____ _____

_____

_____

_____

Year: _____ _____

_____

_____

_____

Year: _____ _____

_____

_____

_____

April 25

What do you want your kid(s) to grow up to be?

Year: _____ _____

_____

_____

_____

Year: _____ _____

_____

_____

_____

Year: _____ _____

_____

_____

_____

Year: _____ _____

_____

_____

_____

Year: _____ _____

_____

_____

_____

April 26

Nothing is more relaxing than the sound of _____.

Year: _____ _____

_____

_____

_____

Year: _____ _____

_____

_____

_____

Year: _____ _____

_____

_____

_____

Year: _____ _____

_____

_____

_____

Year: _____ _____

_____

_____

_____

April 27

What has your child said that warmed your heart?

Year: _____ _____

_____

_____

_____

Year: _____ _____

_____

_____

_____

Year: _____ _____

_____

_____

_____

Year: _____ _____

_____

_____

_____

Year: _____ _____

_____

_____

_____

April 28

How many hugs and kisses did you get today?

Year: _____ _____

_____

_____

_____

Year: _____ _____

_____

_____

_____

Year: _____ _____

_____

_____

_____

Year: _____ _____

_____

_____

_____

Year: _____ _____

_____

_____

_____

April 29

To what are you looking forward?

Year: _____ _____

_____

_____

_____

Year: _____ _____

_____

_____

_____

Year: _____ _____

_____

_____

_____

Year: _____ _____

_____

_____

_____

Year: _____ _____

_____

_____

_____

April 30

To what are your children looking forward?

Year: _____ _____

_____

_____

Year: _____ _____

_____

_____

Year: _____ _____

_____

_____

Year: _____ _____

_____

_____

Year: _____ _____

_____

_____

May 1

Describe a perfect Mother's Day.

Year: _____ _____

_____

_____

_____

Year: _____ _____

_____

_____

_____

Year: _____ _____

_____

_____

_____

Year: _____ _____

_____

_____

_____

Year: _____ _____

_____

_____

_____

May 2

What do you think your neighbors say about you?

Year:_____ _____
_____
_____
_____

Year:_____ _____
_____
_____
_____

Year:_____ _____
_____
_____
_____

Year:_____ _____
_____
_____
_____

Year:_____ _____
_____
_____
_____

May 3

What did not go as planned today?

Year: _____   _____

_____

_____

_____

Year: _____   _____

_____

_____

_____

Year: _____   _____

_____

_____

_____

Year: _____   _____

_____

_____

_____

Year: _____   _____

_____

_____

_____

May 4

Are you a helicopter parent? Explain.

Year: _____ _____

_____

_____

Year: _____ _____

_____

_____

Year: _____ _____

_____

_____

Year: _____ _____

_____

_____

Year: _____ _____

_____

_____

May 5

This is something I hope my kids will say about me:

Year: _____ _____
_____
_____
_____

Year: _____ _____
_____
_____
_____

Year: _____ _____
_____
_____
_____

Year: _____ _____
_____
_____
_____

Year: _____ _____
_____
_____
_____

May 6

What are you trying to let go?

Year: _____   _____

_____

_____

Year: _____   _____

_____

_____

Year: _____   _____

_____

_____

Year: _____   _____

_____

_____

Year: _____   _____

_____

_____

May 7

There are never enough hours in the day to _____.

Year: _____   _____

_____

_____

_____

Year: _____   _____

_____

_____

_____

Year: _____   _____

_____

_____

_____

Year: _____   _____

_____

_____

_____

Year: _____   _____

_____

_____

_____

May 8

I hope my child is a _____ adult.

Year: _____ _____
_____
_____
_____

Year: _____ _____
_____
_____
_____

Year: _____ _____
_____
_____
_____

Year: _____ _____
_____
_____
_____

Year: _____ _____
_____
_____
_____

May 9

For what do you deserve a parenting medal today?

Year: _____ _____

_____

_____

_____

Year: _____ _____

_____

_____

_____

Year: _____ _____

_____

_____

_____

Year: _____ _____

_____

_____

_____

Year: _____ _____

_____

_____

_____

May 10

What energizes you?

Year:_____ _____

_____

_____

_____

Year:_____ _____

_____

_____

_____

Year:_____ _____

_____

_____

_____

Year:_____ _____

_____

_____

_____

Year:_____ _____

_____

_____

_____

May 11

What made you think of your mom lately?

Year: _____   _____
_____
_____
_____

Year: _____   _____
_____
_____
_____

Year: _____   _____
_____
_____
_____

Year: _____   _____
_____
_____
_____

Year: _____   _____
_____
_____
_____

may 12

What made you think of your dad lately?

Year: _____ _____
_____
_____
_____

Year: _____ _____
_____
_____
_____

Year: _____ _____
_____
_____
_____

Year: _____ _____
_____
_____
_____

Year: _____ _____
_____
_____
_____

May 13

What do you wish you had more time to do with your family?

Year:_____ _____
_____
_____
_____

Year:_____ _____
_____
_____
_____

Year:_____ _____
_____
_____
_____

Year:_____ _____
_____
_____
_____

Year:_____ _____
_____
_____
_____

May 14

What difficult questions have your kids asked lately?

Year: _____ _____

_____

_____

Year: _____ _____

_____

_____

Year: _____ _____

_____

_____

Year: _____ _____

_____

_____

Year: _____ _____

_____

_____

May 15

What are you better at now than you were last year?

Year: _____ _____

_____

_____

_____

Year: _____ _____

_____

_____

_____

Year: _____ _____

_____

_____

_____

Year: _____ _____

_____

_____

_____

Year: _____ _____

_____

_____

_____

May 16

What rule(s) do you strictly enforce?

Year: _____ _____

_____

_____

_____

Year: _____ _____

_____

_____

_____

Year: _____ _____

_____

_____

_____

Year: _____ _____

_____

_____

_____

Year: _____ _____

_____

_____

_____

May 17

What rule gets broken again and again in your house?

Year: _____ _____

_____

_____

_____

Year: _____ _____

_____

_____

_____

Year: _____ _____

_____

_____

_____

Year: _____ _____

_____

_____

_____

Year: _____ _____

_____

_____

_____

May 18

What makes you feel complete?

Year: _____   _____

_____

_____

_____

Year: _____   _____

_____

_____

_____

Year: _____   _____

_____

_____

_____

Year: _____   _____

_____

_____

_____

Year: _____   _____

_____

_____

_____

May 19

Describe and rate your last family vacation.

Year: _____   _____

_____

_____

_____

Year: _____   _____

_____

_____

_____

Year: _____   _____

_____

_____

_____

Year: _____   _____

_____

_____

_____

Year: _____   _____

_____

_____

_____

may 20

What three websites do you visit most?

Year: _____ _____

_____

_____

_____

Year: _____ _____

_____

_____

_____

Year: _____ _____

_____

_____

_____

Year: _____ _____

_____

_____

_____

Year: _____ _____

_____

_____

_____

May 21

Describe your love for your child/children.

Year: _____ _____

_____

_____

_____

Year: _____ _____

_____

_____

_____

Year: _____ _____

_____

_____

_____

Year: _____ _____

_____

_____

_____

Year: _____ _____

_____

_____

_____

When do you feel most like yourself?

Year: _____ _____

_____

_____

_____

Year: _____ _____

_____

_____

_____

Year: _____ _____

_____

_____

_____

Year: _____ _____

_____

_____

_____

Year: _____ _____

_____

_____

_____

May 23

What have you sacrificed to become the
parent you want to be?

Year: _____ _____

_____

_____

_____

Year: _____ _____

_____

_____

_____

Year: _____ _____

_____

_____

_____

Year: _____ _____

_____

_____

_____

Year: _____ _____

_____

_____

_____

May 24

How do you define success?

Year: _____ _____

_____

_____

_____

Year: _____ _____

_____

_____

_____

Year: _____ _____

_____

_____

_____

Year: _____ _____

_____

_____

_____

Year: _____ _____

_____

_____

_____

May 25

How have you balanced work and parenting?

Year: _____ _____
_____
_____
_____

Year: _____ _____
_____
_____
_____

Year: _____ _____
_____
_____
_____

Year: _____ _____
_____
_____
_____

Year: _____ _____
_____
_____
_____

May 26

If you were in charge, what law would you pass to help women?

Year: _____ _____
_____
_____
_____

Year: _____ _____
_____
_____
_____

Year: _____ _____
_____
_____
_____

Year: _____ _____
_____
_____
_____

Year: _____ _____
_____
_____
_____

May 27

How will you define your child/children's success?

Year: _____ _____
_____
_____
_____

Year: _____ _____
_____
_____
_____

Year: _____ _____
_____
_____
_____

Year: _____ _____
_____
_____
_____

Year: _____ _____
_____
_____
_____

May 28

What do you wish your child would say to you today?

Year: _____ _____

_____

_____

_____

Year: _____ _____

_____

_____

_____

Year: _____ _____

_____

_____

_____

Year: _____ _____

_____

_____

_____

Year: _____ _____

_____

_____

_____

May 29

What do you wish your partner would say to you today?

Year: _____   _____

_____

_____

_____

Year: _____   _____

_____

_____

_____

Year: _____   _____

_____

_____

_____

Year: _____   _____

_____

_____

_____

Year: _____   _____

_____

_____

_____

May 30

What is your child's most prized possession, and why?

Year: _____ _____

_____

_____

_____

Year: _____ _____

_____

_____

_____

Year: _____ _____

_____

_____

_____

Year: _____ _____

_____

_____

_____

Year: _____ _____

_____

_____

_____

May 31

When have you had to protect your family?

Year: _____ _____

_____

_____

_____

Year: _____ _____

_____

_____

_____

Year: _____ _____

_____

_____

_____

Year: _____ _____

_____

_____

_____

Year: _____ _____

_____

_____

_____

June 1

How do you reward your child/children for good behavior?

Year: _____ _____

_____

_____

_____

Year: _____ _____

_____

_____

_____

Year: _____ _____

_____

_____

_____

Year: _____ _____

_____

_____

_____

Year: _____ _____

_____

_____

_____

June 2

What activates your mother bear instincts?

Year: _____ _____
_____
_____
_____

Year: _____ _____
_____
_____
_____

Year: _____ _____
_____
_____
_____

Year: _____ _____
_____
_____
_____

Year: _____ _____
_____
_____
_____

June 3

What makes you feel beautiful?

Year: _____ _____

_____

_____

_____

Year: _____ _____

_____

_____

_____

Year: _____ _____

_____

_____

_____

Year: _____ _____

_____

_____

_____

Year: _____ _____

_____

_____

_____

June 4

What is your favorite summer activity
to do with your family?

Year: _____ _____

_____

_____

_____

Year: _____ _____

_____

_____

_____

Year: _____ _____

_____

_____

_____

Year: _____ _____

_____

_____

_____

Year: _____ _____

_____

_____

_____

June 5

Which friends help you through hard times?

Year: _____ _____
_____
_____
_____

Year: _____ _____
_____
_____
_____

Year: _____ _____
_____
_____
_____

Year: _____ _____
_____
_____
_____

Year: _____ _____
_____
_____
_____

June 6

Who do you talk to on the phone most often?

Year: _____ _____

_____

_____

_____

Year: _____ _____

_____

_____

_____

Year: _____ _____

_____

_____

_____

Year: _____ _____

_____

_____

_____

Year: _____ _____

_____

_____

_____

June 7

If there were a parenting hotline, how often would you call it?

Year: _____ _____

_____

_____

Year: _____ _____

_____

_____

Year: _____ _____

_____

_____

Year: _____ _____

_____

_____

Year: _____ _____

_____

_____

June 8

Which mom(s) do you trust for advice?

Year:_____ _____

_____

_____

_____

Year:_____ _____

_____

_____

_____

Year:_____ _____

_____

_____

_____

Year:_____ _____

_____

_____

_____

Year:_____ _____

_____

_____

_____

June 9

Which mom(s) drive you crazy, and why?

Year: _____   _____

_____

_____

_____

Year: _____   _____

_____

_____

_____

Year: _____   _____

_____

_____

_____

Year: _____   _____

_____

_____

_____

Year: _____   _____

_____

_____

_____

June 10

When has someone questioned your parenting?

Year: _____ _____

_____

_____

_____

Year: _____ _____

_____

_____

_____

Year: _____ _____

_____

_____

_____

Year: _____ _____

_____

_____

_____

Year: _____ _____

_____

_____

_____

June 11

Which of your kids' friends is your favorite, and why?

Year: _____ _____

_____

_____

_____

Year: _____ _____

_____

_____

_____

Year: _____ _____

_____

_____

_____

Year: _____ _____

_____

_____

_____

Year: _____ _____

_____

_____

_____

June 12

Who is a bad influence on your child?

Year: _____   _____
_____
_____
_____

Year: _____   _____
_____
_____
_____

Year: _____   _____
_____
_____
_____

Year: _____   _____
_____
_____
_____

Year: _____   _____
_____
_____
_____

June 13

What do you understand about your child
that no one else does?

Year: _____ _____

_____

_____

_____

Year: _____ _____

_____

_____

_____

Year: _____ _____

_____

_____

_____

Year: _____ _____

_____

_____

_____

Year: _____ _____

_____

_____

_____

June 14

Who knows your child best?

Year: _____ _____

_____

_____

_____

Year: _____ _____

_____

_____

_____

Year: _____ _____

_____

_____

_____

Year: _____ _____

_____

_____

_____

Year: _____ _____

_____

_____

_____

June 15

When was the last time you lost your temper?

Year: _____ _____

_____

_____

Year: _____ _____

_____

_____

Year: _____ _____

_____

_____

Year: _____ _____

_____

_____

Year: _____ _____

_____

_____

June 16

What is your favorite time of day, and why?

Year: _____ _____
_____
_____
_____

Year: _____ _____
_____
_____
_____

Year: _____ _____
_____
_____
_____

Year: _____ _____
_____
_____
_____

Year: _____ _____
_____
_____
_____

June 17

What struggles do you and your child share?

Year: _____ _____

_____

_____

_____

Year: _____ _____

_____

_____

_____

Year: _____ _____

_____

_____

_____

Year: _____ _____

_____

_____

_____

Year: _____ _____

_____

_____

_____

June 18

What is the best way to help a kid succeed in school?

Year: _____ _____

_____

_____

_____

Year: _____ _____

_____

_____

_____

Year: _____ _____

_____

_____

_____

Year: _____ _____

_____

_____

_____

Year: _____ _____

_____

_____

_____

June 19

If you have free time, what do you usually do with it?

Year: _____ _____

_____

_____

_____

Year: _____ _____

_____

_____

_____

Year: _____ _____

_____

_____

_____

Year: _____ _____

_____

_____

_____

Year: _____ _____

_____

_____

_____

June 20

What do you dream about?

Year: _____ _____

_____

_____

_____

Year: _____ _____

_____

_____

_____

Year: _____ _____

_____

_____

_____

Year: _____ _____

_____

_____

_____

Year: _____ _____

_____

_____

_____

June 21

Write a confession.

Year: _____ _____

_____

_____

_____

Year: _____ _____

_____

_____

_____

Year: _____ _____

_____

_____

_____

Year: _____ _____

_____

_____

_____

Year: _____ _____

_____

_____

_____

June 22

What three things do you value most?

Year: _____   _____

_____

_____

_____

Year: _____   _____

_____

_____

_____

Year: _____   _____

_____

_____

_____

Year: _____   _____

_____

_____

_____

Year: _____   _____

_____

_____

_____

June 23

What three things does your child value most?

Year: _____   _____

_____

_____

Year: _____   _____

_____

_____

Year: _____   _____

_____

_____

Year: _____   _____

_____

_____

Year: _____   _____

_____

_____

June 24

What are the simple pleasures you enjoy?

Year: _____ _____

_____

_____

_____

Year: _____ _____

_____

_____

_____

Year: _____ _____

_____

_____

_____

Year: _____ _____

_____

_____

_____

Year: _____ _____

_____

_____

_____

June 25

What women inspire you?

Year: _____   _____

_____

_____

Year: _____   _____

_____

_____

_____

Year: _____   _____

_____

_____

_____

Year: _____   _____

_____

_____

_____

Year: _____   _____

_____

_____

_____

June 26

What will you never do?

Year: _____ _____

_____

_____

_____

Year: _____ _____

_____

_____

_____

Year: _____ _____

_____

_____

_____

Year: _____ _____

_____

_____

_____

Year: _____ _____

_____

_____

_____

June 27

What is your motto?

Year: _____ _____

_____

_____

_____

Year: _____ _____

_____

_____

_____

Year: _____ _____

_____

_____

_____

Year: _____ _____

_____

_____

_____

Year: _____ _____

_____

_____

_____

June 28

What talents have you honed lately?

Year: _____ _____
_____
_____
_____

Year: _____ _____
_____
_____
_____

Year: _____ _____
_____
_____
_____

Year: _____ _____
_____
_____
_____

Year: _____ _____
_____
_____
_____

June 29

Describe your idea of romance.

Year: _____ _____
_____
_____
_____

Year: _____ _____
_____
_____
_____

Year: _____ _____
_____
_____
_____

Year: _____ _____
_____
_____
_____

Year: _____ _____
_____
_____
_____

June 30

What do very few people know about you?

Year: _____ _____

_____

_____

_____

Year: _____ _____

_____

_____

_____

Year: _____ _____

_____

_____

_____

Year: _____ _____

_____

_____

_____

Year: _____ _____

_____

_____

_____

July 1

What do you wish you cared less about?

Year: _____ _____

_____

_____

_____

Year: _____ _____

_____

_____

_____

Year: _____ _____

_____

_____

_____

Year: _____ _____

_____

_____

_____

Year: _____ _____

_____

_____

_____

July 2

What do you wish you cared more about?

Year: _____ _____

_____

_____

_____

Year: _____ _____

_____

_____

_____

Year: _____ _____

_____

_____

_____

Year: _____ _____

_____

_____

_____

Year: _____ _____

_____

_____

_____

July 3

What makes you feel young?

Year: _____ _____
_____
_____
_____

Year: _____ _____
_____
_____
_____

Year: _____ _____
_____
_____
_____

Year: _____ _____
_____
_____
_____

Year: _____ _____
_____
_____
_____

July 4

What parenting challenges, big or small, did you face today?

Year: _____ _____

_____

_____

_____

Year: _____ _____

_____

_____

_____

Year: _____ _____

_____

_____

_____

Year: _____ _____

_____

_____

_____

Year: _____ _____

_____

_____

_____

July 5

How do you feel about kids and technology?

Year: _____ _____

_____

_____

_____

Year: _____ _____

_____

_____

_____

Year: _____ _____

_____

_____

_____

Year: _____ _____

_____

_____

_____

Year: _____ _____

_____

_____

_____

July 6

What's one thing on your bucket list?

Year: _____ _____

_____

_____

_____

Year: _____ _____

_____

_____

_____

Year: _____ _____

_____

_____

_____

Year: _____ _____

_____

_____

_____

Year: _____ _____

_____

_____

_____

July 7

What new ways have you found to bond with your kids?

Year: _____ _____

_____

_____

_____

Year: _____ _____

_____

_____

_____

Year: _____ _____

_____

_____

_____

Year: _____ _____

_____

_____

_____

Year: _____ _____

_____

_____

_____

July 8

What is the best part about your life?

Year: _____ _____

_____

_____

_____

Year: _____ _____

_____

_____

_____

Year: _____ _____

_____

_____

_____

Year: _____ _____

_____

_____

_____

Year: _____ _____

_____

_____

_____

July 9

If you could have a famous mom over for dinner,
who would you invite?

Year: _____ _____

_____

_____

_____

Year: _____ _____

_____

_____

_____

Year: _____ _____

_____

_____

_____

Year: _____ _____

_____

_____

_____

Year: _____ _____

_____

_____

_____

July 10

When have you doubted yourself?

Year: _____ _____

_____

_____

_____

Year: _____ _____

_____

_____

_____

Year: _____ _____

_____

_____

_____

Year: _____ _____

_____

_____

_____

Year: _____ _____

_____

_____

_____

July 11

What makes your relationship with your kids special?

Year: _____ _____
_____
_____
_____

Year: _____ _____
_____
_____
_____

Year: _____ _____
_____
_____
_____

Year: _____ _____
_____
_____
_____

Year: _____ _____
_____
_____
_____

July 12

What is your ideal weekend?

Year: _____ _____

_____

_____

_____

Year: _____ _____

_____

_____

_____

Year: _____ _____

_____

_____

_____

Year: _____ _____

_____

_____

_____

Year: _____ _____

_____

_____

_____

July 13

What is the best event or party you've attended lately?

Year: _____ _____

_____

_____

_____

Year: _____ _____

_____

_____

_____

Year: _____ _____

_____

_____

_____

Year: _____ _____

_____

_____

_____

Year: _____ _____

_____

_____

_____

July 14

What have you noticed about your child lately?

Year: _____ _____
_____
_____
_____

Year: _____ _____
_____
_____
_____

Year: _____ _____
_____
_____
_____

Year: _____ _____
_____
_____
_____

Year: _____ _____
_____
_____
_____

July 15

What quality are you trying to nurture in your child?

Year: _____ _____

_____

_____

_____

Year: _____ _____

_____

_____

_____

Year: _____ _____

_____

_____

_____

Year: _____ _____

_____

_____

_____

Year: _____ _____

_____

_____

_____

July 16

One year from today, what do you hope your
child/children will have learned?

*Year:*_____　——————————————————

——————————————————————————————————

——————————————————————————————————

——————————————————————————————————

*Year:*_____　——————————————————

——————————————————————————————————

——————————————————————————————————

——————————————————————————————————

*Year:*_____　——————————————————

——————————————————————————————————

——————————————————————————————————

——————————————————————————————————

*Year:*_____　——————————————————

——————————————————————————————————

——————————————————————————————————

——————————————————————————————————

*Year:*_____　——————————————————

——————————————————————————————————

——————————————————————————————————

——————————————————————————————————

July 17

What is today's "quote of the day"?

Year: _____ _____

_____

_____

_____

Year: _____ _____

_____

_____

_____

Year: _____ _____

_____

_____

_____

Year: _____ _____

_____

_____

_____

Year: _____ _____

_____

_____

_____

July 18

When was the last time you had to
speak up for your child?

Year: _____ _____

_____

_____

_____

Year: _____ _____

_____

_____

_____

Year: _____ _____

_____

_____

_____

Year: _____ _____

_____

_____

_____

Year: _____ _____

_____

_____

_____

July 19

When have you had to let go and let
your child handle a problem?

Year: _____ _____

_____

_____

_____

Year: _____ _____

_____

_____

_____

Year: _____ _____

_____

_____

_____

Year: _____ _____

_____

_____

_____

Year: _____ _____

_____

_____

_____

July 20

What was the most exciting thing that happened today?

Year: _____ _____

_____

_____

_____

Year: _____ _____

_____

_____

_____

Year: _____ _____

_____

_____

_____

Year: _____ _____

_____

_____

_____

Year: _____ _____

_____

_____

_____

July 21

What item would you grab if your house were on fire?

Year: _____ _____

_____

_____

_____

Year: _____ _____

_____

_____

_____

Year: _____ _____

_____

_____

_____

Year: _____ _____

_____

_____

_____

Year: _____ _____

_____

_____

_____

July 22

What made you laugh today?

$Year$: _____ _____

_____

_____

_____

$Year$: _____ _____

_____

_____

_____

$Year$: _____ _____

_____

_____

_____

$Year$: _____ _____

_____

_____

_____

$Year$: _____ _____

_____

_____

_____

July 23

How would your child complete this statement:
"My mom is awesome because _____."

Year: _____ _____

_____

_____

_____

Year: _____ _____

_____

_____

_____

Year: _____ _____

_____

_____

_____

Year: _____ _____

_____

_____

_____

Year: _____ _____

_____

_____

_____

July 24

What car suits your personality best?

Year: _____   _____

_____

_____

_____

Year: _____   _____

_____

_____

_____

Year: _____   _____

_____

_____

_____

Year: _____   _____

_____

_____

_____

Year: _____   _____

_____

_____

_____

July 25

What class would you take if you had time?

Year: _____ _____

_____

_____

_____

Year: _____ _____

_____

_____

_____

Year: _____ _____

_____

_____

_____

Year: _____ _____

_____

_____

_____

Year: _____ _____

_____

_____

_____

July 26

What are your strengths as a mom?

Year: _____   _____

_____

_____

_____

Year: _____   _____

_____

_____

_____

Year: _____   _____

_____

_____

_____

Year: _____   _____

_____

_____

_____

Year: _____   _____

_____

_____

_____

July 27

What fantasies have you indulged lately?

Year: _____   _____
_____
_____
_____

Year: _____   _____
_____
_____
_____

Year: _____   _____
_____
_____
_____

Year: _____   _____
_____
_____
_____

Year: _____   _____
_____
_____
_____

July 28

What do you admire most in other people?

Year: _____ _____
_____
_____
_____

Year: _____ _____
_____
_____
_____

Year: _____ _____
_____
_____
_____

Year: _____ _____
_____
_____
_____

Year: _____ _____
_____
_____
_____

July 29

How do you think your kids will describe their childhood?

Year: _____ _____

_____

_____

_____

Year: _____ _____

_____

_____

_____

Year: _____ _____

_____

_____

_____

Year: _____ _____

_____

_____

_____

Year: _____ _____

_____

_____

_____

July 30

What is your newest family tradition?

Year: _____ _____

_____

_____

_____

Year: _____ _____

_____

_____

_____

Year: _____ _____

_____

_____

_____

Year: _____ _____

_____

_____

_____

Year: _____ _____

_____

_____

_____

July 31

How did you celebrate your last birthday?

Year: _____ _____

_____

_____

_____

Year: _____ _____

_____

_____

_____

Year: _____ _____

_____

_____

_____

Year: _____ _____

_____

_____

_____

Year: _____ _____

_____

_____

_____

August 1

When have you stopped to smell the roses lately?

Year: _____ _____
_____
_____
_____

Year: _____ _____
_____
_____
_____

Year: _____ _____
_____
_____
_____

Year: _____ _____
_____
_____
_____

Year: _____ _____
_____
_____
_____

August 2

What do your kids tease you about?

Year: _____ _____

_____

_____

_____

Year: _____ _____

_____

_____

_____

Year: _____ _____

_____

_____

_____

Year: _____ _____

_____

_____

_____

Year: _____ _____

_____

_____

_____

August 3

What is the best part about having kids?

Year: _____ _____

_____

_____

_____

Year: _____ _____

_____

_____

_____

Year: _____ _____

_____

_____

_____

Year: _____ _____

_____

_____

_____

Year: _____ _____

_____

_____

_____

August 4

How would you describe your style?

Year: _____ _____
_____
_____
_____

Year: _____ _____
_____
_____
_____

Year: _____ _____
_____
_____
_____

Year: _____ _____
_____
_____
_____

Year: _____ _____
_____
_____
_____

August 5

What was your last splurge?

Year: _____   _____

_____

_____

_____

Year: _____   _____

_____

_____

_____

Year: _____   _____

_____

_____

_____

Year: _____   _____

_____

_____

_____

Year: _____   _____

_____

_____

_____

August 6

When was the last time you spied on your kids?

Year: _____ _____

_____

_____

_____

Year: _____ _____

_____

_____

_____

Year: _____ _____

_____

_____

_____

Year: _____ _____

_____

_____

_____

Year: _____ _____

_____

_____

_____

August 7

To what extent do you trust your kids?

Year: _____   _____

_____

_____

_____

Year: _____   _____

_____

_____

_____

Year: _____   _____

_____

_____

_____

Year: _____   _____

_____

_____

_____

Year: _____   _____

_____

_____

_____

August 8

What privilege have you taken away from your child?

Year: _____ _____

_____

_____

_____

Year: _____ _____

_____

_____

_____

Year: _____ _____

_____

_____

_____

Year: _____ _____

_____

_____

_____

Year: _____ _____

_____

_____

_____

August 9

What secret do you keep from your kids?

Year: _____ _____

_____

_____

_____

Year: _____ _____

_____

_____

_____

Year: _____ _____

_____

_____

_____

Year: _____ _____

_____

_____

_____

Year: _____ _____

_____

_____

_____

August 10

What makes you feel brave?

Year: _____ _____

_____

_____

_____

Year: _____ _____

_____

_____

_____

Year: _____ _____

_____

_____

_____

Year: _____ _____

_____

_____

_____

Year: _____ _____

_____

_____

_____

August 11

Describe a satisfying parent moment.

Year: _____ _____

_____

_____

_____

Year: _____ _____

_____

_____

_____

Year: _____ _____

_____

_____

_____

Year: _____ _____

_____

_____

_____

Year: _____ _____

_____

_____

_____

August 12

How do you feel about your kids growing up?

Year: _____ _____
_____
_____
_____

Year: _____ _____
_____
_____
_____

Year: _____ _____
_____
_____
_____

Year: _____ _____
_____
_____
_____

Year: _____ _____
_____
_____
_____

August 13

What made you smile today?

Year: _____ _____
_____
_____
_____

Year: _____ _____
_____
_____
_____

Year: _____ _____
_____
_____
_____

Year: _____ _____
_____
_____
_____

Year: _____ _____
_____
_____
_____

August 14

A mother's love is _____.

Year: _____ _____
_____
_____
_____

Year: _____ _____
_____
_____
_____

Year: _____ _____
_____
_____
_____

Year: _____ _____
_____
_____
_____

Year: _____ _____
_____
_____
_____

August 15

What is one bad habit you wish your child could kick?

Year: _____ _____

_____

_____

_____

Year: _____ _____

_____

_____

_____

Year: _____ _____

_____

_____

_____

Year: _____ _____

_____

_____

_____

Year: _____ _____

_____

_____

_____

August 16

What is one bad habit you are trying to kick?

Year: _____ _____

_____

_____

_____

Year: _____ _____

_____

_____

_____

Year: _____ _____

_____

_____

_____

Year: _____ _____

_____

_____

_____

Year: _____ _____

_____

_____

_____

August 17

Do you have any regrets?

Year: _____ _____

_____

_____

_____

Year: _____ _____

_____

_____

_____

Year: _____ _____

_____

_____

_____

Year: _____ _____

_____

_____

_____

Year: _____ _____

_____

_____

_____

August 18

Who truly listens to you?

Year: _____ _____

_____

_____

_____

Year: _____ _____

_____

_____

_____

Year: _____ _____

_____

_____

_____

Year: _____ _____

_____

_____

_____

Year: _____ _____

_____

_____

_____

August 19

Describe a conversation you had recently with your child.

Year: _____ _____

_____

_____

_____

Year: _____ _____

_____

_____

_____

Year: _____ _____

_____

_____

_____

Year: _____ _____

_____

_____

_____

Year: _____ _____

_____

_____

_____

August 20

What emergencies (big or small) have you managed today?

Year: _____ _____

_____

_____

_____

Year: _____ _____

_____

_____

_____

Year: _____ _____

_____

_____

_____

Year: _____ _____

_____

_____

_____

Year: _____ _____

_____

_____

_____

August 21

What is one obstacle your child is facing?

Year: _____ _____

_____

_____

_____

Year: _____ _____

_____

_____

_____

Year: _____ _____

_____

_____

_____

Year: _____ _____

_____

_____

_____

Year: _____ _____

_____

_____

_____

August 22

Who or what is your top priority right now?

Year: _____ _____
_____
_____
_____

Year: _____ _____
_____
_____
_____

Year: _____ _____
_____
_____
_____

Year: _____ _____
_____
_____
_____

Year: _____ _____
_____
_____
_____

August 23

Who has surprised you lately, and why?

Year: _____ _____

_____

_____

_____

Year: _____ _____

_____

_____

_____

Year: _____ _____

_____

_____

_____

Year: _____ _____

_____

_____

_____

Year: _____ _____

_____

_____

_____

August 24

How has your child helped you lately?

Year: _____ _____

_____

_____

_____

Year: _____ _____

_____

_____

_____

Year: _____ _____

_____

_____

_____

Year: _____ _____

_____

_____

_____

Year: _____ _____

_____

_____

_____

August 25

What kind of help would you love to have?

Year: _____ _____

_____

_____

_____

Year: _____ _____

_____

_____

_____

Year: _____ _____

_____

_____

_____

Year: _____ _____

_____

_____

_____

Year: _____ _____

_____

_____

_____

August 26

When have you said no lately?

Year: _____ _____
_____
_____
_____

Year: _____ _____
_____
_____
_____

Year: _____ _____
_____
_____
_____

Year: _____ _____
_____
_____
_____

Year: _____ _____
_____
_____
_____

August 27

What object is most valuable to you right now?

Year: _____ _____

_____

_____

_____

Year: _____ _____

_____

_____

_____

Year: _____ _____

_____

_____

_____

Year: _____ _____

_____

_____

_____

Year: _____ _____

_____

_____

_____

August 28

Where have you had fun taking your child lately?

Year: _____ _____
_____
_____
_____

Year: _____ _____
_____
_____
_____

Year: _____ _____
_____
_____
_____

Year: _____ _____
_____
_____
_____

Year: _____ _____
_____
_____
_____

August 29

How do you do it all?

Year: _____ _____

_____

_____

_____

Year: _____ _____

_____

_____

_____

Year: _____ _____

_____

_____

_____

Year: _____ _____

_____

_____

_____

Year: _____ _____

_____

_____

_____

August 30

What do you hope to pass down to your children?

Year: _____ _____
_____
_____
_____

Year: _____ _____
_____
_____
_____

Year: _____ _____
_____
_____
_____

Year: _____ _____
_____
_____
_____

Year: _____ _____
_____
_____
_____

August 31

What have you overheard your child say lately?

Year: _____ _____

_____

_____

_____

Year: _____ _____

_____

_____

_____

Year: _____ _____

_____

_____

_____

Year: _____ _____

_____

_____

_____

Year: _____ _____

_____

_____

_____

September 1

What family activity do you enjoy in the fall?

Year: _____ _____

_____

_____

_____

Year: _____ _____

_____

_____

_____

Year: _____ _____

_____

_____

_____

Year: _____ _____

_____

_____

_____

Year: _____ _____

_____

_____

_____

September 2

What is the naughtiest thing your child has done?

Year: _____   _____

_____

_____

_____

Year: _____   _____

_____

_____

_____

Year: _____   _____

_____

_____

_____

Year: _____   _____

_____

_____

_____

Year: _____   _____

_____

_____

_____

September 3

What were you able to accomplish today?

Year: _____ _____

_____

_____

_____

Year: _____ _____

_____

_____

_____

Year: _____ _____

_____

_____

_____

Year: _____ _____

_____

_____

_____

Year: _____ _____

_____

_____

_____

September 4

What makes for a good parenting partner?

Year: _____ _____

_____

_____

_____

Year: _____ _____

_____

_____

_____

Year: _____ _____

_____

_____

_____

Year: _____ _____

_____

_____

_____

Year: _____ _____

_____

_____

_____

September 5

If you could give yourself one thing today, what would it be?

Year: _____ _____

_____

_____

_____

Year: _____ _____

_____

_____

_____

Year: _____ _____

_____

_____

_____

Year: _____ _____

_____

_____

_____

Year: _____ _____

_____

_____

_____

September 6

If you could give your family one thing today,
what would it be?

Year: _____ _____

_____

_____

_____

Year: _____ _____

_____

_____

_____

Year: _____ _____

_____

_____

_____

Year: _____ _____

_____

_____

_____

Year: _____ _____

_____

_____

_____

September 7

What are you reading?

Year: _____ _____

_____

_____

_____

Year: _____ _____

_____

_____

_____

Year: _____ _____

_____

_____

_____

Year: _____ _____

_____

_____

_____

Year: _____ _____

_____

_____

_____

September 8

On what do you have the inside scoop?

Year: _____ _____

_____

_____

_____

Year: _____ _____

_____

_____

_____

Year: _____ _____

_____

_____

_____

Year: _____ _____

_____

_____

_____

Year: _____ _____

_____

_____

_____

September 9

What is your superpower?

Year: _____ _____

_____

_____

_____

Year: _____ _____

_____

_____

_____

Year: _____ _____

_____

_____

_____

Year: _____ _____

_____

_____

_____

Year: _____ _____

_____

_____

_____

September 10

Who admires you?

Year: _____ _____
_____
_____
_____

Year: _____ _____
_____
_____
_____

Year: _____ _____
_____
_____
_____

Year: _____ _____
_____
_____
_____

Year: _____ _____
_____
_____
_____

What should everyone do before becoming a parent?

Year: _____ _____
_____
_____
_____

Year: _____ _____
_____
_____
_____

Year: _____ _____
_____
_____
_____

Year: _____ _____
_____
_____
_____

Year: _____ _____
_____
_____
_____

September 12

What have you apologized for recently?

Year: _____ _____

_____

_____

_____

Year: _____ _____

_____

_____

_____

Year: _____ _____

_____

_____

_____

Year: _____ _____

_____

_____

_____

Year: _____ _____

_____

_____

_____

September 13

What are you avoiding doing today?

Year: _____ _____

_____

_____

_____

Year: _____ _____

_____

_____

_____

Year: _____ _____

_____

_____

_____

Year: _____ _____

_____

_____

_____

Year: _____ _____

_____

_____

_____

September 14

What stresses you out most?

Year: _____ _____

_____

_____

_____

Year: _____ _____

_____

_____

_____

Year: _____ _____

_____

_____

_____

Year: _____ _____

_____

_____

_____

Year: _____ _____

_____

_____

_____

September 15

Who is your most trusted friend?

Year: _____ _____

_____

_____

_____

Year: _____ _____

_____

_____

_____

Year: _____ _____

_____

_____

_____

Year: _____ _____

_____

_____

_____

Year: _____ _____

_____

_____

_____

September 16

Siblings are _____.

Year: _____ _____

_____

_____

_____

Year: _____ _____

_____

_____

_____

Year: _____ _____

_____

_____

_____

Year: _____ _____

_____

_____

_____

Year: _____ _____

_____

_____

_____

What makes for a good sibling relationship?

Year: _____ _____

_____

_____

_____

Year: _____ _____

_____

_____

_____

Year: _____ _____

_____

_____

_____

Year: _____ _____

_____

_____

_____

Year: _____ _____

_____

_____

_____

September 18

What are your creative outlets?

Year: _____ _____

_____

_____

_____

Year: _____ _____

_____

_____

_____

Year: _____ _____

_____

_____

_____

Year: _____ _____

_____

_____

_____

Year: _____ _____

_____

_____

_____

September 19

What news did you hear or read today?

Year: _____   _____

_____

_____

_____

Year: _____   _____

_____

_____

_____

Year: _____   _____

_____

_____

_____

Year: _____   _____

_____

_____

_____

Year: _____   _____

_____

_____

_____

September 20

How involved are you in local and/or national politics?

Year: _____ _____
_____
_____
_____

Year: _____ _____
_____
_____
_____

Year: _____ _____
_____
_____
_____

Year: _____ _____
_____
_____
_____

Year: _____ _____
_____
_____
_____

September 21

What causes do you care about most?

Year: _____ _____

_____

_____

_____

Year: _____ _____

_____

_____

_____

Year: _____ _____

_____

_____

_____

Year: _____ _____

_____

_____

_____

Year: _____ _____

_____

_____

_____

September 22

What trouble have you gotten yourself into?

Year: _____ _____

_____

_____

_____

Year: _____ _____

_____

_____

_____

Year: _____ _____

_____

_____

_____

Year: _____ _____

_____

_____

_____

Year: _____ _____

_____

_____

_____

September 23

You haven't lived until you've _____.

Year: _____ _____
_____
_____
_____

Year: _____ _____
_____
_____
_____

Year: _____ _____
_____
_____
_____

Year: _____ _____
_____
_____
_____

Year: _____ _____
_____
_____
_____

September 24

What was the last thing you made?

Year: _____ _____

_____

_____

_____

Year: _____ _____

_____

_____

_____

Year: _____ _____

_____

_____

_____

Year: _____ _____

_____

_____

_____

Year: _____ _____

_____

_____

_____

September 25

How well did your kid(s) listen to you today?

Year: _____ _____

_____

_____

_____

Year: _____ _____

_____

_____

_____

Year: _____ _____

_____

_____

_____

Year: _____ _____

_____

_____

_____

Year: _____ _____

_____

_____

_____

September 26

How much coffee do you need per day?

Year: _____ _____

_____

_____

_____

Year: _____ _____

_____

_____

_____

Year: _____ _____

_____

_____

_____

Year: _____ _____

_____

_____

_____

Year: _____ _____

_____

_____

_____

September 27

Who is the disciplinarian in your house?

Year: _____ _____

_____

_____

_____

Year: _____ _____

_____

_____

_____

Year: _____ _____

_____

_____

_____

Year: _____ _____

_____

_____

_____

Year: _____ _____

_____

_____

_____

September 28

What role does religion play in your life?

Year: _____ _____
_____
_____
_____

Year: _____ _____
_____
_____
_____

Year: _____ _____
_____
_____
_____

Year: _____ _____
_____
_____
_____

Year: _____ _____
_____
_____
_____

September 29

What role does religion play in your child's life?

Year: _____ _____
_____
_____
_____

Year: _____ _____
_____
_____
_____

Year: _____ _____
_____
_____
_____

Year: _____ _____
_____
_____
_____

Year: _____ _____
_____
_____
_____

September 30

Every kid needs a _____.

Year: _____ _____

_____

_____

_____

Year: _____ _____

_____

_____

_____

Year: _____ _____

_____

_____

_____

Year: _____ _____

_____

_____

_____

Year: _____ _____

_____

_____

_____

October 1

To what are you and your partner looking forward?

Year: _____ _____

_____

_____

_____

Year: _____ _____

_____

_____

_____

Year: _____ _____

_____

_____

_____

Year: _____ _____

_____

_____

_____

Year: _____ _____

_____

_____

_____

October 2

If parenting were a school subject,
what part would you be acing?

Year: _____ _____

_____

_____

_____

Year: _____ _____

_____

_____

_____

Year: _____ _____

_____

_____

_____

Year: _____ _____

_____

_____

_____

Year: _____ _____

_____

_____

_____

October 3

If parenting were a school subject,
what part would you be failing?

Year: _____ _____

_____

_____

_____

Year: _____ _____

_____

_____

_____

Year: _____ _____

_____

_____

_____

Year: _____ _____

_____

_____

_____

Year: _____ _____

_____

_____

_____

October 4

How do you and your partner keep the spark alive?

Year: _____ _____

_____

_____

_____

Year: _____ _____

_____

_____

_____

Year: _____ _____

_____

_____

_____

Year: _____ _____

_____

_____

_____

Year: _____ _____

_____

_____

_____

October 5

What is one thing you want to do
with your family today?

Year: _____   _____

_____

_____

_____

Year: _____   _____

_____

_____

_____

Year: _____   _____

_____

_____

_____

Year: _____   _____

_____

_____

_____

Year: _____   _____

_____

_____

_____

October 6

What was the biggest decision you made
for your family this year?

Year: _____   _____

_____

_____

_____

Year: _____   _____

_____

_____

_____

Year: _____   _____

_____

_____

_____

Year: _____   _____

_____

_____

_____

Year: _____   _____

_____

_____

_____

October 7

When the kids have gone to sleep,
what do you enjoy doing?

Year: _____ _____
_____
_____
_____

Year: _____ _____
_____
_____
_____

Year: _____ _____
_____
_____
_____

Year: _____ _____
_____
_____
_____

Year: _____ _____
_____
_____
_____

October 8

What have you lost lately?

Year: _____ _____

_____

_____

_____

Year: _____ _____

_____

_____

_____

Year: _____ _____

_____

_____

_____

Year: _____ _____

_____

_____

_____

Year: _____ _____

_____

_____

_____

October 9

What have you recently found?

Year: _____ _____

_____

_____

_____

Year: _____ _____

_____

_____

_____

Year: _____ _____

_____

_____

_____

Year: _____ _____

_____

_____

_____

Year: _____ _____

_____

_____

_____

October 10

What class would you like to take with your child?

Year: _____ _____

_____

_____

_____

Year: _____ _____

_____

_____

_____

Year: _____ _____

_____

_____

_____

Year: _____ _____

_____

_____

_____

Year: _____ _____

_____

_____

_____

October 11

What has your kid showed you or taught you lately?

Year: _____ _____

_____

_____

_____

Year: _____ _____

_____

_____

_____

Year: _____ _____

_____

_____

_____

Year: _____ _____

_____

_____

_____

Year: _____ _____

_____

_____

_____

October 12

What is the weirdest thing your kid does?

Year: _____ _____

_____

_____

_____

Year: _____ _____

_____

_____

_____

Year: _____ _____

_____

_____

_____

Year: _____ _____

_____

_____

_____

Year: _____ _____

_____

_____

_____

October 13

What is the best thing someone could say about you?

Year: _____ _____

_____

_____

_____

Year: _____ _____

_____

_____

_____

Year: _____ _____

_____

_____

_____

Year: _____ _____

_____

_____

_____

Year: _____ _____

_____

_____

_____

October 14

What is the best thing someone could say about your family?

Year: _____ _____

_____

_____

_____

Year: _____ _____

_____

_____

_____

Year: _____ _____

_____

_____

_____

Year: _____ _____

_____

_____

_____

Year: _____ _____

_____

_____

_____

October 15

_____ fixes everything.

Year: _____ _____

_____

_____

_____

Year: _____ _____

_____

_____

_____

Year: _____ _____

_____

_____

_____

Year: _____ _____

_____

_____

_____

Year: _____ _____

_____

_____

_____

October 16

What was the nicest thing you've ever seen your kid do?

Year: _____ _____

_____

_____

_____

Year: _____ _____

_____

_____

_____

Year: _____ _____

_____

_____

_____

Year: _____ _____

_____

_____

_____

Year: _____ _____

_____

_____

_____

October 17

What is your family's motto?

Year: _____ _____

_____

_____

_____

Year: _____ _____

_____

_____

_____

Year: _____ _____

_____

_____

_____

Year: _____ _____

_____

_____

_____

Year: _____ _____

_____

_____

_____

October 18

What recent experience will you remember forever?

Year: _____   _____
_____
_____
_____

Year: _____   _____
_____
_____
_____

Year: _____   _____
_____
_____
_____

Year: _____   _____
_____
_____
_____

Year: _____   _____
_____
_____
_____

October 19

If you could make more money or enjoy more
free time, which would you choose?

Year: _____ _____

_____

_____

_____

Year: _____ _____

_____

_____

_____

Year: _____ _____

_____

_____

_____

Year: _____ _____

_____

_____

_____

Year: _____ _____

_____

_____

_____

October 20

What was the last brillant idea you had?

Year: _____ _____

_____

_____

_____

Year: _____ _____

_____

_____

_____

Year: _____ _____

_____

_____

_____

Year: _____ _____

_____

_____

_____

Year: _____ _____

_____

_____

_____

October 21

When have you felt rushed lately?

Year: _____ _____

_____

_____

_____

Year: _____ _____

_____

_____

_____

Year: _____ _____

_____

_____

_____

Year: _____ _____

_____

_____

_____

Year: _____ _____

_____

_____

_____

October 22

What's the sneakiest thing you've done lately?

Year: _____ _____

_____

_____

_____

Year: _____ _____

_____

_____

_____

Year: _____ _____

_____

_____

_____

Year: _____ _____

_____

_____

_____

Year: _____ _____

_____

_____

_____

October 23

What is the key to aging gracefully?

Year: _____ _____

_____

_____

_____

Year: _____ _____

_____

_____

_____

Year: _____ _____

_____

_____

_____

Year: _____ _____

_____

_____

_____

Year: _____ _____

_____

_____

_____

October 24

What makes you feel important?

Year: _____ _____

_____

_____

_____

Year: _____ _____

_____

_____

_____

Year: _____ _____

_____

_____

_____

Year: _____ _____

_____

_____

_____

Year: _____ _____

_____

_____

_____

October 25

What historic event(s) occurred recently?

Year: _____   _____
_____
_____
_____

Year: _____   _____
_____
_____
_____

Year: _____   _____
_____
_____
_____

Year: _____   _____
_____
_____
_____

Year: _____   _____
_____
_____
_____

October 26

What big questions do you ask yourself?

Year: _____   _____

_____

_____

_____

Year: _____   _____

_____

_____

_____

Year: _____   _____

_____

_____

_____

Year: _____   _____

_____

_____

_____

Year: _____   _____

_____

_____

_____

October 27

What is the key to happiness?

Year: _____ _____

_____

_____

_____

Year: _____ _____

_____

_____

_____

Year: _____ _____

_____

_____

_____

Year: _____ _____

_____

_____

_____

Year: _____ _____

_____

_____

_____

October 28

How have you improved with age?

Year: _____ _____

_____

_____

_____

Year: _____ _____

_____

_____

_____

Year: _____ _____

_____

_____

_____

Year: _____ _____

_____

_____

_____

Year: _____ _____

_____

_____

October 29

What is your go-to snack food?

Year: _____ _____

_____

_____

_____

Year: _____ _____

_____

_____

_____

Year: _____ _____

_____

_____

_____

Year: _____ _____

_____

_____

_____

Year: _____ _____

_____

_____

_____

October 30

What positive impact have you made on someone's life lately?

Year: _____ _____
_____
_____
_____

Year: _____ _____
_____
_____
_____

Year: _____ _____
_____
_____
_____

Year: _____ _____
_____
_____
_____

Year: _____ _____
_____
_____
_____

October 31

What scares you?

Year: _____ _____

_____

_____

_____

Year: _____ _____

_____

_____

_____

Year: _____ _____

_____

_____

_____

Year: _____ _____

_____

_____

_____

Year: _____ _____

_____

_____

_____

November 1

When does your child really shine?

Year: _____ _____
_____
_____
_____

Year: _____ _____
_____
_____
_____

Year: _____ _____
_____
_____
_____

Year: _____ _____
_____
_____
_____

Year: _____ _____
_____
_____
_____

November 2

I love watching my child when he/she _____ .

Year: _____ _____
_____
_____
_____

Year: _____ _____
_____
_____
_____

Year: _____ _____
_____
_____
_____

Year: _____ _____
_____
_____
_____

Year: _____ _____
_____
_____
_____

November 3

If your family were to break a world record,
which record would it be?

Year: _____ _____

_____

_____

_____

Year: _____ _____

_____

_____

_____

Year: _____ _____

_____

_____

_____

Year: _____ _____

_____

_____

_____

Year: _____ _____

_____

_____

_____

November 4

What milestone did your child reach recently?

Year: _____   _____
_____
_____
_____

Year: _____   _____
_____
_____
_____

Year: _____   _____
_____
_____
_____

Year: _____   _____
_____
_____
_____

Year: _____   _____
_____
_____
_____

When was change difficult for you?

Year: _____   _____
_____
_____
_____

Year: _____   _____
_____
_____
_____

Year: _____   _____
_____
_____
_____

Year: _____   _____
_____
_____
_____

Year: _____   _____
_____
_____
_____

November 6

When have you welcomed change?

Year: _____ _____

_____

_____

_____

Year: _____ _____

_____

_____

_____

Year: _____ _____

_____

_____

_____

Year: _____ _____

_____

_____

_____

Year: _____ _____

_____

_____

_____

If your family could move somewhere new,
where would you go?

Year: _____ _____

_____

_____

_____

Year: _____ _____

_____

_____

_____

Year: _____ _____

_____

_____

_____

Year: _____ _____

_____

_____

_____

Year: _____ _____

_____

_____

_____

November 8

What have you accepted about yourself?

Year: _____ _____

_____

_____

_____

Year: _____ _____

_____

_____

_____

Year: _____ _____

_____

_____

_____

Year: _____ _____

_____

_____

_____

Year: _____ _____

_____

_____

_____

November 9

What have you accepted about your kid(s)?

Year: _____ _____

_____

_____

_____

Year: _____ _____

_____

_____

_____

Year: _____ _____

_____

_____

_____

Year: _____ _____

_____

_____

_____

Year: _____ _____

_____

_____

_____

Are your kids getting easier or more difficult to raise?

Year: _____ _____

_____

_____

_____

Year: _____ _____

_____

_____

_____

Year: _____ _____

_____

_____

_____

Year: _____ _____

_____

_____

_____

Year: _____ _____

_____

_____

_____

November 11

Who would you trust to watch your kid(s) in a pinch?

Year: _____ _____

_____

_____

_____

Year: _____ _____

_____

_____

_____

Year: _____ _____

_____

_____

_____

Year: _____ _____

_____

_____

_____

Year: _____ _____

_____

_____

_____

November 12

What is the best gift you've received lately?

Year: _____ _____

_____

_____

_____

Year: _____ _____

_____

_____

_____

Year: _____ _____

_____

_____

_____

Year: _____ _____

_____

_____

_____

Year: _____ _____

_____

_____

_____

November 13

A _____ a day keeps the doctor away.

Year: _____   _____
_____
_____
_____

Year: _____   _____
_____
_____
_____

Year: _____   _____
_____
_____
_____

Year: _____   _____
_____
_____
_____

Year: _____   _____
_____
_____
_____

November 14

How bright is your future? Describe it.

Year: _____ _____

_____

_____

_____

Year: _____ _____

_____

_____

_____

Year: _____ _____

_____

_____

_____

Year: _____ _____

_____

_____

_____

Year: _____ _____

_____

_____

_____

If you could know one thing about your future,
what would you like to know?

Year: _____ _____

_____

_____

_____

Year: _____ _____

_____

_____

_____

Year: _____ _____

_____

_____

_____

Year: _____ _____

_____

_____

_____

Year: _____ _____

_____

_____

_____

November 16

If you could summarize your day (so far)
in a word, what would it be?

Year: _____ _____

_____

_____

_____

Year: _____ _____

_____

_____

_____

Year: _____ _____

_____

_____

_____

Year: _____ _____

_____

_____

_____

Year: _____ _____

_____

_____

_____

November 17

What is your family's go-to restaurant?

Year: _____ _____

_____

_____

_____

Year: _____ _____

_____

_____

_____

Year: _____ _____

_____

_____

_____

Year: _____ _____

_____

_____

_____

Year: _____ _____

_____

_____

_____

Who is most difficult to get along with in your family?

Year: _____   _____

_____

_____

Year: _____   _____

_____

_____

Year: _____   _____

_____

_____

Year: _____   _____

_____

_____

_____

Year: _____   _____

_____

_____

_____

November 19

What was the last family gathering you attended?

Year: _____ _____

_____

_____

_____

Year: _____ _____

_____

_____

_____

Year: _____ _____

_____

_____

_____

Year: _____ _____

_____

_____

_____

Year: _____ _____

_____

_____

_____

November 20

What made you happy to be a mom today?

Year: _____ _____

_____

_____

_____

Year: _____ _____

_____

_____

_____

Year: _____ _____

_____

_____

_____

Year: _____ _____

_____

_____

_____

Year: _____ _____

_____

_____

_____

When was the last time you multitasked like a champ?

Year: _____ _____

_____

_____

_____

Year: _____ _____

_____

_____

_____

Year: _____ _____

_____

_____

_____

Year: _____ _____

_____

_____

_____

Year: _____ _____

_____

_____

_____

Where do you go for peace and quiet?

Year: _____ _____

_____

_____

Year: _____ _____

_____

_____

Year: _____ _____

_____

_____

Year: _____ _____

_____

_____

Year: _____ _____

_____

_____

November 23

What is the longest you've gone this year
without seeing your kid(s)?

Year: _____ _____

_____

_____

_____

Year: _____ _____

_____

_____

_____

Year: _____ _____

_____

_____

_____

Year: _____ _____

_____

_____

_____

Year: _____ _____

_____

_____

_____

November 24

What makes your child so lovable?

Year: _____ _____
_____
_____
_____

Year: _____ _____
_____
_____
_____

Year: _____ _____
_____
_____
_____

Year: _____ _____
_____
_____
_____

Year: _____ _____
_____
_____
_____

November 25

What is the way to your heart?

Year: _____ _____

_____

_____

_____

Year: _____ _____

_____

_____

_____

Year: _____ _____

_____

_____

_____

Year: _____ _____

_____

_____

_____

Year: _____ _____

_____

_____

_____

November 26

In what area(s) does your child excel?

Year: _____ _____

_____

_____

Year: _____ _____

_____

_____

Year: _____ _____

_____

_____

Year: _____ _____

_____

_____

Year: _____ _____

_____

_____

November 27

What holiday memories have you made this year?

Year: _____   _____

_____

_____

_____

Year: _____   _____

_____

_____

_____

Year: _____   _____

_____

_____

_____

Year: _____   _____

_____

_____

_____

Year: _____   _____

_____

_____

_____

November 28

What do you wish your kid(s) said or did more often?

Year: _____ _____
_____
_____
_____

Year: _____ _____
_____
_____
_____

Year: _____ _____
_____
_____
_____

Year: _____ _____
_____
_____
_____

Year: _____ _____
_____
_____
_____

What time did you enjoy with your child today?

Year: _____ _____

_____

_____

_____

Year: _____ _____

_____

_____

_____

Year: _____ _____

_____

_____

_____

Year: _____ _____

_____

_____

_____

Year: _____ _____

_____

_____

_____

November 30

My kid makes me smile when he/she _____ .

Year: _____ _____

_____

_____

_____

Year: _____ _____

_____

_____

_____

Year: _____ _____

_____

_____

_____

Year: _____ _____

_____

_____

_____

Year: _____ _____

_____

_____

_____

December 1

What is your family's favorite winter activity?

Year: _____ _____

_____

_____

Year: _____ _____

_____

_____

Year: _____ _____

_____

_____

Year: _____ _____

_____

_____

Year: _____ _____

_____

_____

December 2

My kid(s) and I agree on _____.

Year: _____ _____
_____
_____

Year: _____ _____
_____
_____
_____

Year: _____ _____
_____
_____
_____

Year: _____ _____
_____
_____
_____

Year: _____ _____
_____
_____

December 3

Something I'd like to try someday is:

Year:_____   _____
_____
_____
_____

Year:_____   _____
_____
_____
_____

Year:_____   _____
_____
_____
_____

Year:_____   _____
_____
_____
_____

Year:_____   _____
_____
_____
_____

December 4

What are you juggling today?

Year: _____ _____

_____

_____

_____

Year: _____ _____

_____

_____

_____

Year: _____ _____

_____

_____

_____

Year: _____ _____

_____

_____

_____

Year: _____ _____

_____

_____

_____

December 5

If you could meet any friend for coffee and
conversation today, who would it be?

Year: _____   _____

_____

_____

_____

Year: _____   _____

_____

_____

_____

Year: _____   _____

_____

_____

_____

Year: _____   _____

_____

_____

_____

Year: _____   _____

_____

_____

_____

December 6

What are you conflicted about?

Year: _____ _____

_____

_____

_____

Year: _____ _____

_____

_____

_____

Year: _____ _____

_____

_____

_____

Year: _____ _____

_____

_____

_____

Year: _____ _____

_____

_____

_____

December 7

Who have you gotten to know better lately?

Year: _____ _____

_____

_____

_____

Year: _____ _____

_____

_____

_____

Year: _____ _____

_____

_____

_____

Year: _____ _____

_____

_____

_____

Year: _____ _____

_____

_____

_____

December 8

With whom would you want to be marooned on an island?

Year: _____   _____

_____

_____

_____

Year: _____   _____

_____

_____

_____

Year: _____   _____

_____

_____

_____

Year: _____   _____

_____

_____

_____

Year: _____   _____

_____

_____

_____

December 9

When did you last raise your voice?

Year: _____ _____

_____

_____

Year: _____ _____

_____

_____

Year: _____ _____

_____

_____

Year: _____ _____

_____

_____

Year: _____ _____

_____

_____

December 10

Where do you feel most at peace?

Year: _____ _____
_____
_____
_____

Year: _____ _____
_____
_____
_____

Year: _____ _____
_____
_____
_____

Year: _____ _____
_____
_____
_____

Year: _____ _____
_____
_____
_____

December 11

Who do you wish understood your child a little better?

Year: _____ _____

_____

_____

_____

Year: _____ _____

_____

_____

_____

Year: _____ _____

_____

_____

_____

Year: _____ _____

_____

_____

_____

Year: _____ _____

_____

_____

_____

December 12

Who was the last person you called?

Year: _____ _____

_____

_____

_____

Year: _____ _____

_____

_____

_____

Year: _____ _____

_____

_____

_____

Year: _____ _____

_____

_____

_____

Year: _____ _____

_____

_____

_____

December 13

What was the last good piece of mail you received?

Year: _____ _____

_____

_____

_____

Year: _____ _____

_____

_____

_____

Year: _____ _____

_____

_____

_____

Year: _____ _____

_____

_____

_____

Year: _____ _____

_____

_____

_____

December 14

What drives your kid(s) crazy?

Year: _____ _____

_____

_____

_____

Year: _____ _____

_____

_____

_____

Year: _____ _____

_____

_____

_____

Year: _____ _____

_____

_____

_____

Year: _____ _____

_____

_____

_____

December 15

How much time did you spend on social media today?

Year: _____ _____

_____

_____

_____

Year: _____ _____

_____

_____

_____

Year: _____ _____

_____

_____

_____

Year: _____ _____

_____

_____

_____

Year: _____ _____

_____

_____

_____

December 16

What are you excited to teach/show your child next?

Year: _____   _____
_____
_____
_____

Year: _____   _____
_____
_____
_____

Year: _____   _____
_____
_____
_____

Year: _____   _____
_____
_____
_____

Year: _____   _____
_____
_____
_____

December 17

What white lie have you told your child lately?

Year: _____ _____

_____

_____

_____

Year: _____ _____

_____

_____

_____

Year: _____ _____

_____

_____

_____

Year: _____ _____

_____

_____

_____

Year: _____ _____

_____

_____

_____

December 18

When have you had good luck?

Year: _____ _____

_____

_____

Year: _____ _____

_____

_____

Year: _____ _____

_____

_____

Year: _____ _____

_____

_____

Year: _____ _____

_____

_____

December 19

When have you had bad luck?

Year: _____ _____

_____

_____

_____

Year: _____ _____

_____

_____

_____

Year: _____ _____

_____

_____

_____

Year: _____ _____

_____

_____

_____

Year: _____ _____

_____

_____

_____

December 20

If you wrote a book about your parenting experience
this year, what would the title be?

Year: _____   _____

_____

_____

_____

Year: _____   _____

_____

_____

_____

Year: _____   _____

_____

_____

_____

Year: _____   _____

_____

_____

_____

Year: _____   _____

_____

_____

_____

December 21

Make a promise to yourself today and write it below.

Year: _____ _____

_____

_____

_____

Year: _____ _____

_____

_____

_____

Year: _____ _____

_____

_____

_____

Year: _____ _____

_____

_____

_____

Year: _____ _____

_____

_____

_____

December 22

Make a promise to your child and write it below.

Year: _____ _____

_____

_____

_____

Year: _____ _____

_____

_____

_____

Year: _____ _____

_____

_____

_____

Year: _____ _____

_____

_____

_____

Year: _____ _____

_____

_____

_____

December 23

What is new in your life?

Year: _____ _____

_____

_____

_____

Year: _____ _____

_____

_____

_____

Year: _____ _____

_____

_____

_____

Year: _____ _____

_____

_____

_____

Year: _____ _____

_____

_____

_____

December 24

If you could freeze one moment of this day,
what moment would it be?

Year: _____ _____

_____

_____

_____

Year: _____ _____

_____

_____

_____

Year: _____ _____

_____

_____

_____

Year: _____ _____

_____

_____

_____

Year: _____ _____

_____

_____

_____

December 25

What are you grateful for today?

Year: _____ _____

_____

_____

_____

Year: _____ _____

_____

_____

_____

Year: _____ _____

_____

_____

_____

Year: _____ _____

_____

_____

_____

Year: _____ _____

_____

_____

_____

December 26

What excites you?

Year: _____ _____

_____

_____

_____

Year: _____ _____

_____

_____

_____

Year: _____ _____

_____

_____

_____

Year: _____ _____

_____

_____

_____

Year: _____ _____

_____

_____

_____

December 27

Life is a _____.

Year: _____ _____

_____

_____

_____

Year: _____ _____

_____

_____

_____

Year: _____ _____

_____

_____

_____

Year: _____ _____

_____

_____

_____

Year: _____ _____

_____

_____

_____

December 28

Describe a time when you trusted your instincts.

Year: _____ _____

_____

_____

_____

Year: _____ _____

_____

_____

_____

Year: _____ _____

_____

_____

_____

Year: _____ _____

_____

_____

_____

Year: _____ _____

_____

_____

_____

December 29

What reaffirms your decision to become a mom?

Year: _____ _____

_____

_____

Year: _____ _____

_____

_____

Year: _____ _____

_____

_____

Year: _____ _____

_____

_____

Year: _____ _____

_____

_____

December 30

How do you keep your family together?

Year: _____ _____

_____

_____

_____

Year: _____ _____

_____

_____

_____

Year: _____ _____

_____

_____

_____

Year: _____ _____

_____

_____

_____

Year: _____ _____

_____

_____

_____

December 31

My advice for moms-to-be is:

Year: _____ _____

_____

_____

_____

Year: _____ _____

_____

_____

_____

Year: _____ _____

_____

_____

_____

Year: _____ _____

_____

_____

_____

Year: _____ _____

_____

_____

_____